Library of Congress Cataloging-in-Publication Data available

ISBN 0-439-33731-3

10 9 8 7 6 5 4 3 2 1   01 02 03 04 05

Printed in the U.S.A.

First printing, November 2001

"Why do fireflies glow?"

...and other

Questions Kids Ask™

About
Crawly Creatures

📖 SCHOLASTIC

New York   Toronto   London   Auckland   Sydney
Mexico City   New Delhi   Hong Kong   Buenos Aires

TABLE OF CONTENTS

QUESTIONS KIDS ASK ABOUT CRAWLY CREATURES

Dear QKA Reader,

I love insects and spiders. They're delicious! For a lizard like me, fresh, crunchy bugs are fine dining.

Most humans don't eat bugs, but I know you think they're interesting. Even I have to admit that insects and spiders have some unusual talents. Fireflies can glow in the dark, which is a pretty cool skill to have. And how about spiders? Where in the world do they learn how to weave those webs?

Even though I'd still rather eat them than watch them, I do have a lot to learn about insects and spiders. Maybe you do, too. That's why this book is devoted to answering your questions about the world's "crawly creatures."

Read on! And keep on asking questions.

Your pondering pal,

Leonardo da Lizard

P.S. I love to hunt for insects and spiders! Look for me creeping around throughout the pages of this book!

The smallest known adult insect is a fairy fly. The fairy fly is a kind of parasitic wasp. Parasites depend on other plants or animals, called hosts, to live. The fairy fly lives and feeds on the eggs of other insects.

The fairy fly is so small, it wasn't discovered until 1997. It can only be seen through a microscope. The female is 1/125 inch (.02 cm) long. The adult male fairy fly is blind and wingless and even smaller.

So far, only the females of certain other parasitic wasps have been identified. It could be that the males are just too small to be seen. So, it's likely that there are even smaller insects than the fairy fly just waiting to be discovered.

What's the smallest insect in the world?

It's so small, you really can't see it.

EXTRA

The smallest beetle is the feather-winged beetle. It is smaller than the period at the end of this sentence. The tiniest moth is even smaller: Found in England, it has a wingspan of 1/100 of an inch (.025 mm)!

The world's largest beetle is the Hercules beetle. It can grow to be 7 inches (18 cm) from the tip of its jaws to the end of its body. That's a bit longer than the length of this yellow box! The Hercules' larva, the immature, worm-like stage of its development, can be as long as 10 inches (25 cm).

Africa's Goliath beetle is the world's heaviest flying insect. It can weigh as much as 8 1/2 ounces (241 g). Goliaths feed on dead plant material and animal droppings. These big bugs are in the scarab family of beetles. They have beautiful, bright shell patterns.

The world's longest insect is the giant walking stick. A giant walking stick can grow to 12 inches (30 cm) from nose to tail. These insects look like sticks, so they can easily hide on tree branches, blending in to protect themselves from predators.

What's the biggest beetle in the world?

It's so BIG, they named it after Hercules.

OK, so show me where your problem is.

Big Old Bug

Scientists have found fossils of cockroaches far bigger than the Hercules beetle. The fossils are from the Jurassic period, when dinosaurs roamed the Earth.

Why aren't spiders considered insects?

There are some telltale differences.

Spiders are not insects, but insects and spiders are related. Spiders and insects are both arthropods—animals with segmented bodies, hard outside coverings, and no backbones. However, spiders and insects have many differences.

Ordinarily, spiders have eight simple eyes. Each of these eyes has one lens. Some insects have simple eyes, but many have two compound eyes. Each of these eyes can have hundreds or even thousands of lenses.

Another feature that some spiders have but insects don't is pedipalps. Pedipalps look like two arms sticking out above the legs. They are used to bite, grasp, or touch.

Spider versus Insect
The main differences between insects and spiders are:

Spiders	Insects	Spiders	Insects
Two body segments	Three body segments	Have pedipalps	No pedipalps
Four pairs of legs	Three pairs of legs	No wings	Can have wings
Can have fangs	No fangs	No antennae	Most have antennae
Eat insects	Most eat plants	Simple eyes	Can have compound or simple eyes

What are spiders' closest relatives?

Eight-legged creepy-crawlies belong to this family.

Spiders are arachnids not insects, so their closest relatives are not bees and ants, but scorpions, ticks, mites, and harvestmen (also called daddy longlegs). There are approximately 74,000 known species of arachnids, and scientists believe there are still more to be discovered.

Arachnids usually have eight legs and two body segments; though some, such as ticks and mites, have one body segment.

Most arachnids live on land, and nearly all are meat-eating animals called carnivores. Arachnids' diet consists mainly of insects and small animals.

EXTRA

The long, tall legs of daddy longlegs protect them from small enemies closer to the ground, such as ants. They can shed a leg to avoid capture by a predator, and then grow it back later! Unlike spiders, they don't spin webs.

Spiders' Relatives

Scorpions	Tips of their tails contain a poisonous stinger
Ticks and mites	Small bloodsucking parasites that live off of other animals
Harvestmen (Daddy longlegs)	Have small rounded bodies and are often mistaken for spiders

When two ants meet, they touch each other with their antennae. Ants can learn almost as much with just their antennae as you can with your five senses!

But ants can't see with their antennae. Some researchers think that the ants use their sense of smell to recognize one another. Scientists think that each ant nest may have a special smell, and the ants from that nest all smell the same.

Ants don't like trespassers. In fact, an ant colony may claim and defend a territory of thousands of square yards. So if two ants from different colonies meet, they'll probably fight. But if they're from the same colony, they're very hospitable. One of them may even "feed" the other by regurgitating a drop of liquid into its mouth.

12

How do ants recognize each other?

"How do you do? I smell you."

Don't invite them to your picnic!

Bulldog ants	Large and fierce
Army ants	Tropical raiders and swarmers
Fire ants	Have painful stings
Harvester ants	Carry grain
Leaf-cutter ants	Grow fungus to eat
Carpenter ants	Chew nests in trees

Unlike many kinds of ants, army ants from Central and South America (also called driver ants) don't make hills or nests. Instead, they travel from place to place in a big group called a colony. A colony may have more than 1.5 million ants—sometimes up to 20 million!

Army ants travel because they need food. Newly hatched ants, called larvae, eat a great deal as they grow. When the young ants grow up, they don't eat as much. Then the colony stops for about three weeks while the queen lays eggs. After the eggs hatch, the colony moves on. The adults carry the new larvae as they travel.

As army ants march through villages, people who live there actually leave their houses. When the people return, they find all their food, plants, and garbage eaten by the ant colony.

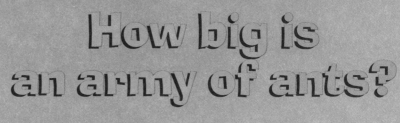

How big is an army of ants?

It's bigger than the population of many cities!

EXTRA

When the *Eciton* species of army ants stops to rest, ants cling together in a great ball, called a bivouac, with the queen and the young in the middle. This species of ant is native to South America.

Do bedbugs really crawl in your bed?

Sleep tight; they're probably not in yours.

Fill 'er up

Talk about a nightmare! Bedbugs didn't get their name by accident. These icky little insects can live in cracks and crevices around the house. Mattresses are among their favorite hiding places.

Tiny, flat bedbugs bite animals—including humans—and suck their blood. They seem to be highly sensitive to temperature, and it's possible that bedbugs find their prey simply by detecting the warmth of animals' bodies.

Bedbugs don't fly, but they can run very fast. They come out at night and scope out their territory, then they feed in the early morning hours when people are asleep. While common in the past, it's less likely that your home would have bedbugs today.

EXTRA
The largest bedbugs grow to be only ½ inch (1.3 cm) long. Many are less than ¼ in (.6 cm) long.

Before they feed, bedbugs are almost completely flat. As they fill up on blood, the bugs plump up.

Do earwigs really crawl in your ears?

They're more likely to crawl into your garden.

EXTRA

Most earwigs have wings, but they rarely use them.

Gettin' Earwiggy

There are 18 species of earwigs found in North America, including:

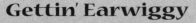

Black earwigs

Seaside earwigs

Striped earwigs

Little earwigs

Long-Horned earwigs

Handsome earwigs

Maybe the story about earwigs crawling into people's ears was made up by parents trying to get their kids to wash. Just thinking about these ugly insects, with their sharp pincers, rummaging around in your ear should make you reach for soap and water!

Earwigs are active at night. During the day, they hide under piles of trash. At night, they come out to feed on plants and debris. If threatened, earwigs will use their pincer tails to pinch their attackers. And some species will shoot a smelly liquid from their abdomens.

But as far as scientists know, earwigs don't have any special fondness for nesting in people's ears. So, now you can relax. There's no truth to the story about earwigs. (But you still have to clean your ears!)

When a female mosquito stabs you with her mouthparts—only the females sting—she injects you with a chemical that makes it easier for her to sip your blood. It's this chemical, found in the female mosquito's saliva, that makes you itch. After she injects the chemical, the mosquito sips your blood. Your blood provides nourishment for the eggs developing inside her body.

Mosquitoes are really types of flies. Of the 3,000 kinds of mosquitoes, only a few feed off humans and animals. Some of these are of special concern, however, because they can spread diseases.

Why do mosquito bites itch?
A nasty chemical can really get under your skin.

ITCHING POWDER

16

Mosquito Facts

Wings	2	Eggs laid	100–300 at a time, 3,000 in a lifetime
Body parts	3	Life span	
Life stages	4	Males	7–10 days
		Females	30+ days; some live during the winter

There are different types of flies—including mosquitoes and tsetse flies. But they all have at least one thing in common: sucking mouthparts.

A fly places a drop of digestive liquid on its food before it eats it. This liquid acts the way the acid in your stomach breaks down food. The fly then sucks the liquid and some of the broken-down food into its body through its mouthpart.

Houseflies love to chow on garbage, human and animal waste, and other not-so-appealing stuff. But that doesn't mean they won't eat other types of food, such as a bit of your sandwich! So, you should be sure to keep your food, especially meat and fruit, covered if you hear flies buzzing around. You don't want them leaving disease-causing germs on food you're going to eat!

How do flies eat?

They use a built-in straw.

Fly, Fly Away!

- The average housefly flaps its wings 200 times every second.
- A housefly's eyes are made up of over 4,000 tiny surfaces.
- Houseflies can walk on windows and ceilings probably because of liquid that comes out from little pads beneath the claws on their feet.

17

How many insects live on Earth?

Bet you can't count this high!

There are more species of insects than all animal species put together. At least 1 million different species of insects are present on Earth. And, that's just the number that scientists know about. Most scientists who study insects say there are millions more that they haven't found and named yet.

And speaking of high numbers, scientists estimate that there are about 10 quintillion (10,000,000,000,000,000,000!) insects alive on Earth at any time. This means, there are approximately 100 million insects for every person. You can think of it this way— insects have you outnumbered 100 million to 1!

Insects also are some of the toughest creatures on Earth. They can live almost anywhere, no matter what the climate. In fact, some insects survive at the South Pole!

EXTRA

Scientists who study insects are called entomologists. The name comes from the Greek word *entomon*, which means "insect." Discovering a new species of insect can be the happiest event in an entomologist's career.

What insect has the biggest population on Earth?

No other bug can beat the beetle!

BUG CENSUS BUREAU

There are more types, or species, of beetles than any other insect on Earth. Scientists have counted more than 300,000 species of beetles in the world and 23,000 different species in the United States alone. And one in every four animals on Earth is a beetle.

Some beetles are super-huge. The acteon beetle from South America can be almost 4 inches (9 cm) long, and the South American longhorn beetle grows to be more than 6 inches (16 cm) long. That's about the length of your pencil!

Other beetles are really tiny. For instance, the feather-winged beetle from North America is smaller than a pencil eraser.

EXTRA
Some beetles live in the water of lakes and ponds. They can swim, dive, and hunt underwater. Some water beetles can even eat fish or frogs.

19

Honey is made by honeybees. Worker honeybees spend their days traveling from flower to flower, using their long tongues to suck up each flower's nectar. The nectar is then stored in a pouch inside the bees' bodies. Bees also collect pollen, which they pack into tiny basket-like structures on their back legs. After visiting up to 100 flowers, the honeybees return to the hive.

The honeybees' hive is made of honeycomb, which is built of wax. The bees produce the wax with their bodies. After they return home from a day's work, the bees spit up, or regurgitate, the nectar they've collected. Some of the nectar is then placed in honeycomb cells, where it turns into honey for future use. Other nectar is mixed with the flower pollen and made into bee bread. This "bread" is fed to baby honeybees, called larvae.

20

How do bees make honey?

It's a team effort.

Honeybee, make honey for me!
Honeybee facts:

- When worker honeybees find a place with lots of flowers they like, they return to the hive and do a special dance. This dance tells the other bees where the flowers are.
- The worker bees look after the queen bee, who lays all the eggs for the hive.
- A honeybee has two pairs of wings.
- Sometimes, the pollen falls off the bee into another flower. This is the way honeybees help pollinate plants.

A queen bee is the leader of the honeybee hive. Even though her only job is to lay eggs, it is an exhausting daily task. The queen uses a scent called a pheromone to keep other female bees from being able to lay eggs. Single-handedly, she rules a group, or colony, of tens of thousands of honeybees.

The male bees in the colony are called drones, and their job is to mate with the queen so she can continue to lay eggs. The female bees in the colony, other than the queen, are worker bees. They have many jobs. The workers take care of the queen, defend the colony, collect pollen and nectar, and make honey. Workers also build the honeycomb cells, where honey and pollen are stored and the queen's eggs develop into adult bees.

What makes the "queen bee" the queen?
Her majesty keeps the family growing.

EXTRA

A queen bee lives from 1–7 years. During that time, she can lay up to 1,500 eggs a day. That means she may lay more than 3,800,000 eggs in her lifetime!

Wee Eggs

The queen's eggs are so tiny that one of them could fit on the dot of this i.

What's the difference between moths and butterflies?

They're like night and day.

This question is tricky because, in fact, moths and butterflies are more alike than they are different. Both moths and butterflies have two sets of feathery wings (most insects have just one set). Adult moths and butterflies both have long tube-shaped tongues that they use to suck nectar from plants. And both moths and butterflies develop from caterpillars.

Scientists have come up with a few guidelines for separating the butterflies from the moths, but there are plenty of exceptions. Generally, butterflies are brightly colored insects that are active during the day. When they rest, butterflies spread their wings apart. Butterflies' antennae are usually rounded at the ends.

Moths are usually dull-colored and are active at night. When they rest, moths close their wings. Their antennae are usually narrow at the ends.

Why do moths fly around lights?

They're confused by the brightness.

Spot the Differences

Moths	Butterflies
Fly at night	Fly by day
Usually dull-colored	Brightly colored
Feathery antennae	Clubbed antennae
Rest with wings closed	Rest with wings spread

Moths use light from the moon and stars to find their way at night. These light rays come from very far away and reach each of a moth's eyes with equal brightness. Exposed to this light, the moth can stay balanced and fly a straight path.

But light rays from nearby porch lamps or other artificial sources reach a moth's eyes differently. Artificial light appears brighter to one of the moth's eyes than to the other. So the moth becomes off-balance. On one side, its wings move faster than on the other, causing the doomed insect to spin and then spiral right into the light.

Moths aren't the only insects attracted to artificial light. Certain kinds of beetles are also likely to flit around outdoor lights.

EXTRA
There are more than 200,000 known species of moths and butterflies.

On warm summer evenings in some places, the air comes alive with the sound of crickets. But it's only the male crickets making all the noise. They are trying to attract female crickets with their mating calls. It may sound as if they're singing in a chorus, but actually, they're trying to "outchirp" each other. The louder the crickets chirp, the more likely they are to attract mates.

A male cricket chirps by rubbing one wing over the other. The underside of each wing has a rough, narrow strip called a file. The cricket rubs this file over another rough part, called a scraper, located on the upper surface of the other wing. When a female cricket appears, the male's song quickly changes. Once the male is sure he's found his mate, he changes his tune into a quiet, gentle song.

24

Why do crickets chirp?

These sounds are special messages.

EXTRA

Some people believe crickets are temperature indicators. They suggest that you count the number of chirps in 15 seconds and add 40 to give you the approximate temperature in degrees Fahrenheit.

Keep on Chirping

In the Chesapeake region of the eastern United States, crickets are regarded as wise souls. An old tale says it's bad luck when a cricket in the house stops chirping.

A firefly's abdomen contains special cells, which contain certain chemicals. When these chemicals combine with oxygen and other chemicals, light is given off. Scientists call this process bioluminescence.

The fireflies you see blinking around at night are most likely the males. The females are sitting in the brush waiting to flash their lights in response. This is how the males find their mates. Fireflies also use their flashing light to warn other fireflies of danger. The amount of oxygen they let into their abdomens controls the brightness of the glow.

The light is also helpful in discouraging predators. The chemicals that go into making its glow taste bad. When predators see the light, they know to stay away.

Why do fireflies glow?

There's a signal in each sparkle.

EXTRA

There are more than 170 species of fireflies in the United States and 1,900 in the world. Fireflies, often called lightning bugs, are neither flies nor bugs. They're beetles.

You light up my life
Other creatures that glow are:

Flashlight fish

Angler fish

Luminous bacteria

Glowworm caterpillar

25

Do centipedes really have 100 legs?

Hmm. Someone should check the math.

Sizing up Centipedes
Centipedes vary widely in size:

Scutigera forceps, the "house centipede," can be 1 to 2 inches (2.5–5 cm) long. The West Indies' *Scolopendra giganteas*, the largest known centipede, can be up to 12 inches (30 cm) long.

Although the word *centipede* means "hundred feet or legs," most centipedes don't quite live up to the name. *Scutigera forceps*, the common house centipede that you might find in your basement, has only 15 pairs of legs (30 legs in all). Its two front limbs aren't even used for walking—they're actually fangs. The centipede uses these limbs to grab and poison small insects for food.

Different centipede species have varying numbers of body segments, each with its own pair of legs. Most centipedes are born with only a few segments, growing new ones as they age. They do this by repeatedly dividing their rear segments into two. This allows some centipedes to sprout as many as 354 limbs! But whether they have 30 legs or 300, centipedes can use them with great coordination and speed.

Do stink bugs stink?

The truth hurts— it also smells terrible.

Stink bugs have earned their reputation. When these bugs are disturbed, they give off a distinctly foul odor. In other words, they stink! The odor comes from stink glands in the bug's upper body, called the thorax.

While their smell is their most notable characteristic, stink bugs have even more unpleasant features. Many species are plant eaters with huge appetites. They like to eat food crops, such as peas, beans, soybeans, and fruit. Using their long, pointed "beaks," plant-eating stink bugs suck the juice out of plant stems, seeds, and fruits. They'll also chow down on cotton crops and cause enormous damage. Farmers really think stink bugs stink!

EXTRA

In North America, stink bugs are found mainly in the southern U.S. The little shield-shaped, flat-backed bugs grow to be about .47 inches (1.2 cm) long.

27

Some members of the insect world are great home builders. Mud daubers build nests from mud. Females stack balls of mud to make long, skinny tubes. Then they stuff dead bugs inside the tubes. Next, females will lay one egg in each tube. When the eggs hatch, they feed on the dead prey.

Paper wasps work as a team to chew up bits of wood fiber and spit it out into a white papery substance. They use this substance to build a nest. One 8-inch (20-cm)-wide nest may be home to 200 paper wasps.

Termites in Africa and Australia use hard balls of dirt and saliva to build huge mounds, which hold tens of thousands of termites. Most termite mounds are taller than a grown man, and some are taller than the trees around them!

How do bugs build their homes?

They don't use hammers and nails.

EXTRA
The biggest termite mound in the world was found in Australia. It was 20 feet (6 m) tall and measured 100 feet (30 m) across at the base.

Bees sting to protect themselves and their hives. If you don't bother them, they will usually leave you alone. Actually, only certain kinds of bees sting. The most common are honeybees and bumblebees. And they pay a high price for stinging you. Their stingers have hook-like edges, so the bees can't pull them out after they have stung an animal or person. When the bee pulls away, the stinger is ripped off, and the bee dies.

Only female bees sting. That's because the stinger is part of the egg-laying organ of a bee, which males don't have.

Although they aren't bees, yellow jackets, other wasps, and hornets also have stingers. But they can pull their stingers out of a person's skin and use them over and over again. So bee-ware!

Why do bees sting?

Bee-ware! They're serious about self-defense.

EXTRA

Scientists are testing whether bee venom, the poison that bees inject when they sting, may be helpful in treating certain diseases.

Bee Facts

Eyes 5	Legs 6	Wings 4
Flight speed		22 miles per hour (35 kph)
Flight distance		8 miles (13 km)
Life span		Workers 7–8 weeks
Queens		2–7 years
First bees		About 146 to 174 million years ago

29

Why do fleas like dogs?

Your pooch's fur says, "Welcome here."

FLEA CIRCUS

If you were a flea, you might look at a dog and think, "Yum! Dinner!" That's because fleas feed on dogs. They bite into their skin and suck their blood. That's how fleas get their nutrients. No wonder fleas can be dogs' worst enemy.

Fleas can feed on any warm-blooded animal, even humans! A cat flea can consume more than 15 times its body weight in cat blood every day.

Fleas can't fly, but they're excellent jumpers. If they need to leave one animal host, they just jump off and find another. Fleas have been known to jump 150 times their own length. That means tiny fleas measuring about 3/16 inch (.05 mm) can jump more than 28 inches (71 cm). Whee!

Fleas can't stand freezing temperatures. That's why pets aren't bothered during cold winters, but as the temperatures rise— look out!

What's the difference between a flea and a tick?

One's an insect, and one isn't.

There's a big difference between fleas and ticks. Fleas are insects. Ticks are not.

Ticks have eight legs. That means they are part of the group called arachnids, along with spiders and scorpions. All insects have six legs. No more. No less.

Even so, ticks still "bug" animals and humans the way fleas do. Ticks bite into their skin and feed on their blood. They also carry diseases that can be quite dangerous to humans and animals.

Ticks have been around for a long time. In early 2001, archaeologists found the world's oldest tick. It was preserved in amber from the Cretaceous Period. It could be 90 million years old.

Why do ladybugs have spots?

Pretty polka dots provide defense.

The spots, along with their bright red, orange, or yellow shells, warn potential **predators**: Ladybugs taste awful! If their spots don't frighten animals away, ladybugs defend themselves by squirting blood from their leg joints. This blood contains a very stinky, foul-tasting substance. Once birds, ants, and spiders find this out, they never forget it!

Usually, ladybugs in the same species have the same number of spots on their wing covers. But there are over 4,000 different kinds of ladybugs in the world—with more than 150 different species in the United States.

EXTRA

Ladybugs, also called ladybirds, are natural pest controllers. They eat tiny insects called aphids. Aphids can destroy a whole crop by sucking the juices from plants' leaves. But not with ladybugs around!

How did the praying mantis get its name?

Its looks got the name, but its hunger got the fame.

Waiting patiently for a juicy spider, beetle, or other insect to wander by, the praying mantis keeps its powerful front limbs folded together. This position makes it look like the mantis is praying, which is where the name "praying mantis" comes from.

Really, the other bugs should be saying their prayers. Those nasty front limbs are equipped with spines to hold their prey while the mantis squeezes and bites into its bug lunch.

The sneaky mantis uses camouflage to help trap its prey. For instance, the snazzy pink and green flower mantis hides among the tropical flowers in its habitat. Other species of mantis look like leaves or twigs. So, unsuspecting bugs never even know when there's a mantis around.

EXTRA

The word mantis comes from the Greek word for prophet or seer. Ancient Greeks believed the mantis had the power to predict the future.

Hide Me!

Camouflage helps the mantis fool predators. Birds and bats love to eat mantises—when they can find them!

There are chompers and borers.

EXTRA

Carpenter bees are black and yellow, like bumble bees. Females can sting, but males can't.

34

Termites are the world's most infamous wood-eating insects. They feed on the cellulose fiber, which is found in wood pulp. Most of the time they eat dead wood, such as old, rotten tree trunks. But, sometimes they find their way into the wooden beams of houses. Then watch out! A colony of termites will eat until the wood falls apart.

Some other insects don't actually eat wood. They just tunnel through it. Carpenter ants build colonies in rotting logs and stumps. They've also been known to nest in houses, and even in telephone poles! Inside the wood, they build a series of tunnels. They don't eat the wood, they just pile it outside the entry to the tunnel.

Carpenter bees are another type of wood-chewing insect. They bore perfectly round holes in moist or soft wood and keep on tunneling, leaving little piles of sawdust behind them.

How long does it take a spider to spin a web?

It's surprising how quickly things can get sticky.

Large and Small Webs

Tropical spiders of the genus *Nephila* spin the largest webs. They're more than 18 feet (5 m) around. The smallest webs are spun by the *Glyphesis cottonae*. They cover less than 1 square inch (6 square cm).

In less than one hour, a spider can spin a delicate web out of silk to trap unsuspecting insects. A spider releases the silk through six spinnerets, which are organs in its abdomen. This silk dribbles out as a liquid and hardens upon contact with the air. Depending on the spider's needs, it can produce dry or sticky silk strands, ranging from very fine to quite thick.

Many spiders weave bicycle-wheel-like webs. They use dry thread for the center and spokes, and sticky thread for the circles that spiral out from the center. Other types of spiders spin simple single-thread webs or funnel-shaped webs.

No matter the shape, insects and other prey stick to the gooey web. But slippery oil on the spider's "feet" keeps it from getting caught in its own trap.

EXTRA
The average spider has to replace its web every few days because it loses its stickiness.

There are more than a few animals that like to eat spiders. To avoid being another creature's lunch, spiders defend themselves in various ways.

Most spiders have a poisonous bite. They bite and injure a predator to avoid being eaten themselves.

Other spiders have built-in disguises, or camouflage. For example, in New Guinea, South America, there's a type of crab spider with a shiny, wet-looking body that makes it look like bird droppings.

Some spiders will also try to run away from their enemies. Nursery-web spiders can run across the surface of a pond or stream, or even go underwater to escape!

Spiders have a way of making sure that future generations of spiders survive. They lay lots of eggs. This increases the chance that plenty of baby spiders reach adulthood.

36

How do spiders defend themselves?

They use fright, flight, and bite.

Are tarantulas dangerous?

Tarantulas are hairy, have fangs, and can be quite big. Scary? Maybe. Dangerous? To most humans, no.

To begin with, a tarantula probably won't bite unless it is bothered. More likely, it will run away. If you were bitten by a tarantula, you'd feel a little pain (but not a lot), and there might be a little swelling around the bite. You probably wouldn't get sick, though.

Tarantulas have venom, which they use to stun their prey, but it's too weak to affect humans (except for some people who are severely allergic). Some of the tarantulas found in India, Sri Lanka, and Africa are more dangerous than those that live in the United States, however.

Their looks are scarier than their bite!

Toads Beware!

EXTRA
Tarantula bites have not caused any human deaths in recorded history.

Most tarantulas live in burrows underground and catch their prey by hunting it down. They are nocturnal—in other words, they go out at night and sleep during the day. Insects are their main food, but some larger tarantulas can devour toads—and even small birds or snakes!

Where do insects go in winter?

It's time for a bug holiday.

It's cold outside!
Insect methods of winter survival:

Tent caterpillar	Egg
Elm-leaf beetle	Hibernation
Tomato hornworm	Pupa
Monarch butterfly	Migration

Have you ever had to come in from ice-skating because of all those pesky mosquitoes? Of course not! But insects don't disappear or die in winter. Nature has just given them clever ways to wait out the cold.

For many insects, winter brings a change in their appearance. Some insects spend the winter as thick-shelled eggs, which provide insulation from the cold. Others change back to an immature form, such as a larva or pupa.

Still others hibernate in their adult forms, finding cozy little nooks in houses or trees. Bees huddle in their hives where they keep warm by vibrating their wings. Insects that don't change form or hibernate often travel, or migrate, to warmer places. Monarch butterflies, which fly to Mexico or Southern California, are an example of the insect world's vacationers.

How does a caterpillar turn into a butterfly?

It's all part of growing up.

When it is young, a caterpillar spends its time chewing on leaves and other plant materials. Some caterpillars eat a lot in their short lives.

Then one day, the caterpillar stops eating and prepares to go through a change in its life. First the caterpillar sticks itself to a leaf or stem. Then it sheds its skin and forms a new hard outer coating called a chrysalis. The chrysalis protects the caterpillar as its body continues to change. At this stage in its life, the caterpillar is known as a pupa.

Inside the chrysalis, the pupa grows and changes shape. In a few weeks, wings start to form. Then, finally, the pupa is ready to pop out of the chrysalis. When it does, all traces of the caterpillar are gone. And, there's a beautiful butterfly or moth in its place.

Boll weevils are beetles that feed on cotton plants. They live in Mexico and in the southern United States, where cotton is an important crop. Because of their huge appetites, boll weevils are dreaded by cotton farmers.

Boll weevils are also called snout beetles. That's because they have long, thin noses, or snouts, which they use to puncture a cotton plant's seed pod and suck out its fibers. The cotton plant's seed pod is called a boll. That's how the boll weevil got its name.

Farmers really hate these little bugs. If boll weevils infest a cotton crop, they can completely destroy it. Every year, about 8 percent of the cotton crop in the United States is lost to hungry, destructive boll weevils.

What do boll weevils eat?

Evil weevils consume cotton.

EXTRA

Boll weevils are only about 1/8 inch (3 mm) to 5/16 inch (8.5 mm) in size. It's hard to believe such small bugs can do such big damage!

MENU

DRIVE IN

COTTON FLUFF
AIR CONE
PUFF
COTTON BURST
PINKY

Locusts are grasshoppers with unusual habits. Most of the time, locusts live alone and feed on plants. But when locusts run out of food, trouble starts. They join together in huge groups, called swarms, and go in search of plants to eat.

One swarm may include 80 million locusts. It looks like a huge black cloud, and can travel more than 80 miles (130 km) in one day. When the swarm finds new plants to eat, look out! The locusts will eat every plant in sight. No wonder farmers fear them!

Each locust can eat its body weight in food every day. That's about .07 ounces (2 g) of food per locust. It doesn't sound like much until you multiply the number by 80 million. Yikes! A swarm of locusts can eat as much in one day as 10 elephants or 2,500 people.

What kind of insect is a locust?

It's a grasshopper with a mammoth appetite.

EXTRA

Locusts live in dry regions of Africa, the Middle East, and southwestern Asia. Swarms of locusts often cross the Red Sea, between Egypt and Saudi Arabia.

41

Dragonflies don't look like dragons. But the combination of the way they fly and the way they swoop may have led people to compare them to the dragons of fairytales.

Equipped with four independent wings, dragonflies can fly forward, backward, and hover in midair. They are often brightly colored and shiny. When they spot an insect meal, they swoop in quickly, snatching their prey out of the air.

Dragonflies and their close relatives, the smaller damselflies, belong to the insect order Odonata. *Odonata* is a Greek word that means "toothed one." This refers to the saw-like teeth located on dragonflies' chewing mouth parts, or mandibles.

EXTRA

Scientists have discovered more than 5,000 species of dragonflies worldwide, including 450 in North America.

Do dragonflies really look like dragons?

Not exactly, but there is some resemblance.

Around the U.S.
Other names for dragonflies include:

Section of U.S.	Dragonflies' names
South	Snake doctors
Midlands	Snake feeder
South Atlantic	Skeeter hawks
Upper North	Darning needles
Coastal New Jersey	Spindles
Northern	California ear sewers

QUESTIONS KIDS ASK ABOUT CRAWLY CREATURES

abdomen [AB-duh-men] the hind part of the body of an insect

aphid [AY-fid] a variety of tiny soft-bodied insects that suck the juices from plants

arachnids [uh-RAK-nuhdz] animals, such as spiders and scorpions, with eight legs but no antennae

bioluminescence [beye-oh-luh-muh-NE-suhns] the process by which such animals as fireflies and glowworms produce light

bivouac [BI-vuh-wak] the great ball that Eciton army ants form while resting, in which they surround the queen and the young in the middle

camouflage [KA-muh-floj] the way specific species of animals, such as the praying mantis and stick insect, look like their surroundings and therefore blend in as a form of defense against predators

carnivore [KOR-nuh-vohr] a meat-eating animal

cellulose [SEL-yuh-lohs] a plant or wood fiber that certain insects, such as termites, feed on

chrysalis [KRI-suh-les] the pupa stage of the development of a moth or butterfly that is enclosed in a firm protective case

cocoon [kuh-KOON] a protective casing in the pupa stage of an insect's development

colony [KO-luh-nee] a group of one species of animals, such as bees and ants, that live together

drone [drohn] a male bee

entomologist [en-tuh-MO-luh-jist] a scientist who studies insects

hibernate [HI-buhr-nayt] to become inactive; when an animal's heart rate and breathing slow down for a period of time so that the animal can survive difficult conditions, such as an extremely cold winter

infest [in-FEST] to spread or swarm in a troublesome way

larva [LOR-vuh] an early form of any animal that at birth or hatching is very different from its parents

lens [lenz] a part of an animal's eye that focuses light to form clear images

mandible [MAN-duh-buhl] the chewing mouth parts in some animals, such as dragonflies

migrate [MEYE-grayt] to move from one place to another

nocturnal [nok-TER-nuhl] active at night

nourishment [NER-ish-muhnt] something, such as healthy food, that sustains an animal

parasite [PAR-uh-seyet] an animal that lives in or on some other living thing and gets food, and often shelter, from it

pheromone [FER-uh-mohn] a substance given off by many animal species, as in the scent used by a queen honeybee to rule, or dominate, her colony

pedipalp [PE-duh-palp] a pair of limbs of an arachnid near the mouth that has a special purpose, such as biting or touching

pollinate [po-luh-NAY-shuhn] to transfer pollen from one flower to other flowers as bees do

QUESTIONS KIDS ASK ABOUT CRAWLY CREATURES

predator [PRE-duh-ter] an animal that hunts other animals

pupa [PYU-puh] an intermediate inactive stage of an insect's development during which the insect is inside a cocoon or other protective covering

regurgitate [ree-GER-juh-tayt] when some animals, such as ants and bees, cast up food to feed their young or others of their species

spinneret [spi-nuh-RET] an organ in a spider or caterpillar that makes threads of silk

thorax [thor-AKS] the middle of the three main parts of an insect's body

venom [VE-nuhm] poisonous matter produced by some animals to use on their prey or enemies; usually by biting or stinging

QUESTIONS KIDS ASK ABOUT CRAWLY CREATURES